YOUR FIRST FIVE YEARS

YOUR FIRST FIVE YEARS

BABY MEMORY BOOK

Terri McHugh

R ROCKRIDGE PRESS

First Rockridge Press trade paperback edition 2023

Rockridge Press and the Rockridge Press logo are trademarks or registered trademarks of Callisto Media Inc. and/or its affiliates in the United States and other countries and may not be used without written permission.

For general information on our other products and services, please contact our Customer Care Department within the United States at (866) 744-2665, or outside the United States at (510) 253-0500.

Hardcover ISBN: 979-8-88650-227-5

Manufactured in the United States of America

Interior and Cover Designer: John Calmeyer
Art Producer: Cristina Coppin
Editor: Kahlil Thomas
Production Editor: Ashley Polikoff
Production Manager: Lanore Coloprisco

Illustrations © Illuztrate/ Creative Market with the following exceptions: Shutterstock: © pikepicture: 2, © Olha Kozachenko: (first and second birthday sections); author photo courtesy of Liam McHugh

10 9 8 7 6 5 4 3 2 1 0

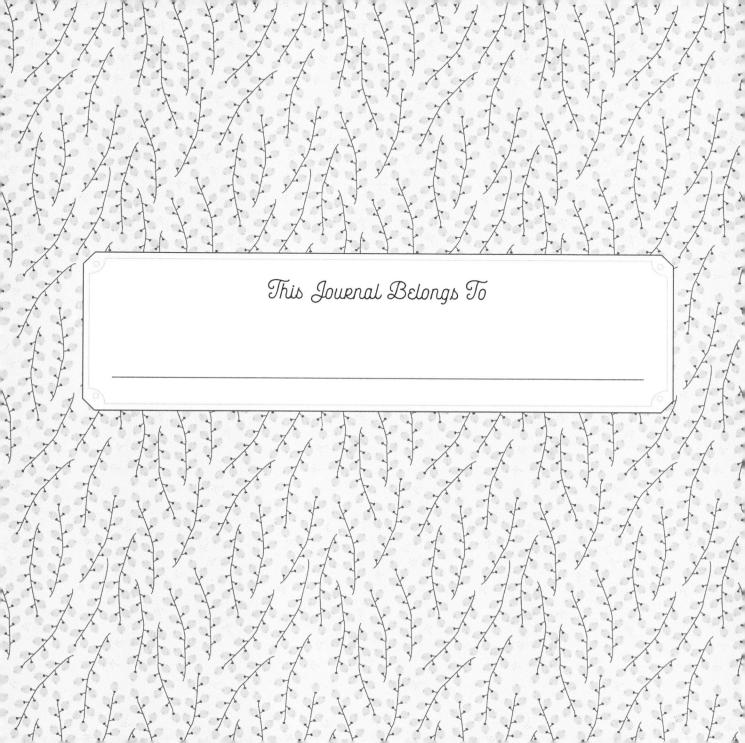

This Journal Belongs To

CONTENTS

Watch with glittering eyes the whole world around you because the greatest secrets are always hidden in the most unlikely places.

—ROALD DAHL

WELCOME TO YOUR BABY MEMORY BOOK!

This book will come along for the ride as you embark on your journey into parenthood. Here you will capture all the moments that tell the story of your family throughout your child's first five years. All caregivers are encouraged to use this book and hold on to it as a special keepsake for the years to come. Whether you're a first-time parent or have been down this road before, whatever the dynamic of your family unit may be, this book was made for anyone and everyone in mind.

Life can easily become too busy, and moments we hope to remember slip away from us. That is what makes this baby memory book so special. It will tell the story only you can tell. This is the place where you can log special moments and collect the images and mementos that will build your story. As you begin using your baby memory book, you will notice it is designed to record experiences from early infancy up to five years of age. Each portion of this memory book is meant to progress along with you from the days leading up to baby's arrival through the toddler years.

In this book, you will find pages filled with guiding prompts, memento sections that allow you to insert photos and write down ideas, as well as blank areas you can customize. The moments you choose to record will become an invaluable keepsake for you and your child. You're the author that will tell this story, an incredibly special story unlike any other. Don't be afraid to reflect on your emotions as you begin to fill out these pages. It will remind you of where you were when you look back through your personal notes in the months and years to come. I'm so excited for you to start this adventure and create something special that will be a treasure for you and your loved ones! And I hope this book fills your heart with joy every time you pick it up.

OUR FAMILY TREE

BEFORE YOU ARRIVED

The days leading up to your arrival have been busy, little one! From the moment your presence was known up until now, a lot has taken place. *Some of the most memorable experiences preparing for you have included*

_____

_____

_____

_____

_____

_____

_____

_____

_____

_____

_____

_____

_____

_____

_____

CELEBRATING YOUR ARRIVAL

Your arrival was a cause for celebration! Gathering your baby items was such an important task. *One fun way your arrival was celebrated was*

_____

_____

_____

_____

_____

_____

_____

_____

_____

_____

_____

_____

_____

_____

THE STORY OF YOUR BIRTH

THE DAY YOU CAME HOME

You're home! *Our first moments together at home were*

_____

_____

_____

_____

_____

_____

_____

_____

_____

_____

_____

_____

Your name is _____

You were born on _____ at _____ and weighed _____
(DATE) (TIME)

Your eye color is _____

Your hair color is _____

A LETTER TO WELCOME YOU

_____

_____

_____

_____

_____

_____

_____

_____

_____

_____

_____

_____

_____

_____

_____

_____

YOUR BABY'S FIRST TWELVE MONTHS

Welcome to the first twelve months! This is the first year of a five-year journey that is unlike any other. The months in your child's first year of life are full of moments worth capturing and milestones you'll want to remember. Here you'll find pages filled with prompts that will encourage you to jot down the growth and experiences your child encounters, month to month. You will have the opportunity to record the exact dates, locations, and events in which these milestones and special moments took place.

You'll also be able to add personal notes and photos as sweet mementos you'll love to look back on. The first twelve months may have many sleepless nights and demanding days, but they'll also contain an unexplainable joy you will always remember. Try to capture it all as you fill in the blanks to tell your story.

Piglet sighed with happiness, and began to think about himself. He was BRAVE...

—A. A. MILNE

Your baby is not the only one with big feelings. Most likely, you have experienced several of your own. Share a few thoughts on what this first month has been like for you.

_____

_____

_____

_____

_____

_____

_____

_____

_____

_____

_____

_____

_____

_____

_____

_____

A month can feel like it goes by quickly for some people and way too slowly for others. How would you describe this time in your baby's life? Is it moving too quickly or too slowly?

_____

_____

_____

_____

_____

_____

_____

_____

_____

_____

_____

_____

_____

_____

_____

_____

In the first few months of life, you may have seen some changes that provided you with glimpses into your child's personality. What have you seen so far?

_____

_____

_____

_____

_____

_____

_____

_____

_____

_____

_____

_____

_____

_____

_____

Every child develops at their own pace. What are some milestone "firsts," if any, you've seen your child hitting during these months?

_____

_____

_____

_____

_____

_____

_____

_____

_____

_____

_____

_____

_____

_____

_____

_____

_____

Life is full of surprises. Have situations during this time surprised you as a parent? Any experiences or emotions you did not anticipate? Have your expectations differed from reality, and if so, how?

_____

_____

_____

_____

_____

_____

_____

_____

_____

_____

_____

_____

_____

_____

_____

Based on your experience so far, what thoughts would you offer someone wanting to become a parent? Advice, encouragement, warnings?

_____

_____

_____

_____

_____

_____

_____

_____

_____

_____

_____

_____

_____

_____

_____

_____

_____

It's all about the little details. What routine with the baby has become a major part of your day? It could be bath time, tummy time, a stroll around the block, etc. What makes it important?

_____

_____

_____

_____

_____

_____

_____

_____

_____

_____

_____

_____

_____

_____

Babies have a way of modifying how we do things and how we live life. What would you say has changed the most in your day to day? Has adapting been easy or difficult?

_____

_____

_____

_____

_____

_____

_____

_____

_____

_____

_____

_____

_____

_____

_____

_____

What is the most meaningful thing you've seen your baby do so far? A first smile or wave, an awareness in their gaze, a discovery of bath bubbles? Describe it below.

_____

_____

_____

_____

_____

_____

_____

_____

_____

_____

_____

_____

_____

_____

_____

_____

_____

MOMENTS OF REFLECTION

During these months you have learned a lot about your child, including the little things that make your baby smile or feel irritated. Share some memorable moments, good or bad, that have given you added insight into parenthood.

_____

_____

_____

_____

_____

_____

_____

_____

_____

_____

_____

_____

_____

_____

_____

_____

They say it takes a village to raise a child. Have you found that to be true? Are there other people involved in your child's life that are playing a major role in their upbringing?

_____

_____

_____

_____

_____

_____

_____

_____

_____

_____

_____

_____

_____

_____

_____

MAJOR MILESTONES

The first time you smiled _____

_____

_____

_____

_____

_____

_____

_____

When you first sat up _____

_____

_____

_____

_____

_____

_____

_____

_____

_____

MAJOR MILESTONES

When you found your feet _____

_____

_____

_____

_____

_____

_____

_____

When you started teething _____

_____

_____

_____

_____

_____

_____

_____

_____

MAJOR MILESTONES

When you waved hello or goodbye _____

_____

_____

_____

_____

_____

_____

_____

The day you first giggled _____

_____

_____

_____

_____

_____

_____

_____

_____

MAJOR MILESTONES

When you seem to get annoyed _____

_____

_____

_____

_____

_____

_____

_____

The item that soothes you most _____

_____

_____

_____

_____

_____

_____

_____

_____

MAJOR MILESTONES

When you like to nap _____

_____

_____

_____

_____

_____

_____

_____

When you are the happiest _____

_____

_____

_____

_____

_____

_____

_____

_____

MAJOR MILESTONES

When you first slept through the night _____

_____

_____

_____

_____

_____

_____

_____

The first solid food you ate _____

_____

_____

_____

_____

_____

_____

_____

_____

Favorite solid food _____

_____

_____

_____

_____

_____

_____

_____

Your least favorite solid food _____

_____

_____

_____

_____

_____

_____

_____

MAJOR MILESTONES

The first time you clapped _____

_____

_____

_____

_____

_____

_____

_____

When you first rolled over _____

_____

_____

_____

_____

_____

_____

_____

MAJOR MILESTONES

Your first favorite toy _____

_____

_____

_____

_____

_____

_____

_____

_____

When you first held something _____

_____

_____

_____

_____

_____

_____

_____

_____

_____

MAJOR MILESTONES

Your first favorite person to see _____

_____

_____

_____

_____

_____

_____

_____

Your first favorite song _____

_____

_____

_____

_____

_____

_____

_____

_____

MAJOR MILESTONES

Your favorite fictional character _____

_____

_____

_____

_____

_____

_____

_____

_____

When you pulled yourself up _____

_____

_____

_____

_____

_____

_____

_____

_____

MAJOR MILESTONES

When you stood up _____

_____

_____

_____

_____

_____

_____

_____

When you tried to take a step _____

_____

_____

_____

_____

_____

_____

_____

MONTH-TO-MONTH CHANGES

It's hard to see growth and changes happening right before your eyes, especially if those changes are subtle at times. In this section, you are encouraged to write out the month-to-month changes that can be visibly seen when compared to one another. You'll be able to record transformations in height and weight, as well as include the kind of growth you are looking forward to in the month that follows. By the time you reach the final entry in this portion of the book, you will be able to compare the differences that took place each month over your baby's first year.

Month _____   Height _____

Date _____   Weight _____

How You've Changed from Last Month

_____

_____

What I'm Looking Forward to Next Month

_____

_____

My Memories from This Month

_____

_____

_____

_____

_____

PHOTO

Month _____   Height _____

Date _____   Weight _____

How You've Changed from Last Month

_____

_____

What I'm Looking Forward to Next Month

_____

_____

My Memories from This Month

_____

_____

_____

_____

_____

PHOTO

Month _____   Height _____

Date _____   Weight _____

How You've Changed from Last Month

_____

_____

What I'm Looking Forward to Next Month

_____

_____

My Memories from This Month

_____

_____

_____

_____

_____

PHOTO

Month _____ Height _____

Date _____ Weight _____

How You've Changed from Last Month

_____

_____

What I'm Looking Forward to Next Month

_____

_____

My Memories from This Month

_____

_____

_____

_____

_____

PHOTO

Month _____ Height _____

Date _____ Weight _____

How You've Changed from Last Month

_____

_____

What I'm Looking Forward to Next Month

_____

_____

My Memories from This Month

_____

_____

_____

_____

_____

PHOTO

43

Month _____   Height _____

Date _____   Weight _____

How You've Changed from Last Month

_____

_____

What I'm Looking Forward to Next Month

_____

_____

My Memories from This Month

_____

_____

_____

_____

_____

PHOTO

Month _____   Height _____

Date _____   Weight _____

How You've Changed from Last Month

_____

_____

What I'm Looking Forward to Next Month

_____

_____

My Memories from This Month

_____

_____

_____

_____

_____

PHOTO

47

Month _____   Height _____

Date _____   Weight _____

How You've Changed from Last Month

_____

_____

What I'm Looking Forward to Next Month

_____

_____

My Memories from This Month

_____

_____

_____

_____

_____

PHOTO

Month _____   Height _____

Date _____   Weight _____

How You've Changed from Last Month

_____

_____

What I'm Looking Forward to Next Month

_____

_____

My Memories from This Month

_____

_____

_____

_____

_____

PHOTO

51

Month _____   Height _____

Date _____   Weight _____

How You've Changed from Last Month

_____

_____

What I'm Looking Forward to Next Month

_____

_____

My Memories from This Month

_____

_____

_____

_____

_____

PHOTO

Month _____ Height _____

Date _____ Weight _____

How You've Changed from Last Month

_____

_____

What I'm Looking Forward to Next Month

_____

_____

My Memories from This Month

_____

_____

_____

_____

_____

PHOTO

Month _____   *Height* _____

Date _____   *Weight* _____

How You've Changed from Last Month

_____

_____

What I'm Looking Forward to Next Month

_____

_____

My Memories from This Month

_____

_____

_____

_____

_____

PHOTO

YOUR FIRST WORDS AND EXPRESSIONS

You're communicating! The cooing started when _____

_____

_____

I saw you smile when _____

_____

_____

You make funny gestures when _____

_____

_____

You make babbling sounds when _____

_____

_____

The first word you spoke was _____

_____

_____

YOUR FAVORITE THINGS

Your favorite thing to do _____

_____

_____

Your favorite thing that I do _____

_____

_____

Your most prized possession _____

_____

_____

Your favorite food to snack on _____

_____

_____

Your favorite game to play (like peekaboo) _____

_____

_____

A LETTER TO YOU AT SIX MONTHS

LOOKING BACK ON YOUR FIRST TWELVE MONTHS

Today you are you! That is truer than true! There is no one alive who is you-er than you! Shout loud, "I am lucky to be what I am!"

—DR. SEUSS

YOUR CHILD IS ONE!

Congratulations! The first year has come and gone. The first twelve months are officially under your belt. Get ready for the toddler years. Take this time to celebrate this year through a collection of highlighted moments you'll record in these pages and reflect on throughout the years. You will have a chance to log important events like your child's first birthday, milestones, and memorable occasions.

Now is a good time to pull out baby photos and birthday cards, along with other special souvenirs and treasures you can stick onto a page. In this section, you will find blank areas you can fill with special memento photographs, notes, or other items to preserve as keepsakes for your child, like ticket stubs or a flower from their favorite plant. Be as creative and detailed as you like.

CELEBRATING YOUR FIRST BIRTHDAY

You're one! How we celebrated

_____

_____

The people that were there

_____

_____

The fun presents you received

_____

_____

What you loved eating

_____

_____

The activities on this day

_____

_____

Your baby has experienced so many changes in the last year. How has watching your baby grow month to month made you feel? Share some thoughts you have reflected on in these last twelve months.

_____

_____

_____

_____

_____

_____

_____

_____

_____

_____

_____

_____

_____

_____

_____

_____

Raising a baby can have its victories as well as its challenges. What has your experience been this year? Share accomplishments you're most proud of or possible challenges that helped you grow as a parent.

_____

_____

_____

_____

_____

_____

_____

_____

_____

_____

_____

_____

_____

_____

_____

_____

MOMENTS OF REFLECTION

What valuable lesson have you learned in the last twelve months that you will carry with you throughout the journey of parenthood? Take time to reflect and share a few thoughts on those transformative moments.

_____

_____

_____

_____

_____

_____

_____

_____

_____

_____

_____

_____

_____

_____

_____

_____

As you think back on this first year of raising your baby, which month(s) would you say stood out as an all-time favorite? Share some examples of what made that time memorable and enjoyable.

_____

_____

_____

_____

_____

_____

_____

_____

_____

_____

_____

_____

_____

_____

_____

_____

It is not always rainbows and butterflies in the life of a parent, and that is okay! Share some examples of those challenging moments. What has made those phases difficult and what has helped (or is helping) you overcome it?

As much as you've gotten to know your baby, you've also learned a lot about who you are as a parent. What would you say you learned to lean into as a motto for raising your child?

_____

_____

_____

_____

_____

_____

_____

_____

_____

_____

_____

_____

_____

_____

_____

_____

MAJOR MILESTONES

The first time you self-fed _____

_____

_____

_____

_____

_____

_____

_____

The first steps you took _____

_____

_____

_____

_____

_____

_____

_____

_____

MAJOR MILESTONES

Your first reaction to walking _____

_____

_____

_____

_____

_____

_____

_____

My thoughts when you walked _____

_____

_____

_____

_____

_____

_____

_____

MAJOR MILESTONES

The day you recognized your name _____

_____

_____

_____

_____

_____

_____

_____

When you tried to dance _____

_____

_____

_____

_____

_____

_____

_____

_____

MAJOR MILESTONES

The first game you played _____

_____

_____

_____

_____

_____

_____

_____

Your favorite thing to do outside _____

_____

_____

_____

_____

_____

_____

_____

_____

WHAT YOU SAID

The first word you ever said _____

_____

_____

Your favorite word to say _____

_____

_____

My favorite word you say _____

_____

_____

Words you understand _____

_____

_____

When you see _____ , you say _____

_____!

YOUR FAVORITE THINGS

Your most prized possession

_____

_____

Your favorite food to eat

_____

_____

Your favorite game to play

_____

_____

Your favorite people to see

_____

_____

Your favorite sound to hear

_____

_____

A LETTER TO YOU AT ONE

LOOKING BACK ON YOUR FIRST YEAR

It is only with the heart that one can see clearly. What is essential is invisible to the eye.

—ANTOINE DE SAINT-EXUPÉRY

YOUR CHILD IS TWO!

Time to celebrate! Your child is two, can you believe it? Once a baby, now a toddler, with new milestones and experiences to write about. In this portion of the book, you will be encouraged to expound on the prompts given on each page, with categories ranging from new phrases spoken and favorite toys played with to closest friends made in this last year. The more details you remember to share, the better the story you will be able to tell. The little nuances of what seem to be ordinary days have a way of holding a special place in our hearts. Your child's favorite cartoon of the moment or their favorite cup to drink from—those simple details will color your story beautifully. No need to rush and answer questions quickly; this is the time to savor your child's second year of life and share the moments that had an impact.

CELEBRATING YOUR SECOND BIRTHDAY

How you celebrated your birthday

_____

_____

What you loved eating

_____

_____

The people who celebrated with you

_____

_____

Your favorite gift

_____

_____

The outfit you wore

_____

_____

Are the clichés true? Has your child entered the "terrible twos" phase? Share your experiences raising a toddler. What differences (if any) have you seen in this last year in comparison to year one?

_____

_____

_____

_____

_____

_____

_____

_____

_____

_____

_____

_____

_____

_____

_____

_____

_____

_____

Watching your little one grow from a baby to a toddler can produce certain emotions as you see this change take place. Share some thoughts that describe your overall feelings throughout this second year.

_____

_____

_____

_____

_____

_____

_____

_____

_____

_____

_____

_____

_____

_____

_____

Each season brings new experiences and milestones. What have you seen in your child's second year of life that you have been excited about? What are you looking forward to?

_____

_____

_____

_____

_____

_____

_____

_____

_____

_____

_____

_____

_____

_____

_____

_____

_____

_____

It can be said that wisdom and certain parenting skills can be acquired with experience. Do you agree? What unique insight have you gained from parenting a two-year-old? How are your own skills developing?

_____

_____

_____

_____

_____

_____

_____

_____

_____

_____

_____

_____

_____

_____

_____

MAJOR MILESTONES

When you laugh the most _____

_____

_____

_____

_____

_____

_____

_____

_____

When you love to hug _____

_____

_____

_____

_____

_____

_____

_____

_____

_____

MAJOR MILESTONES

When you stood on your tiptoes _____

_____

_____

_____

_____

_____

_____

_____

When you threw a ball _____

_____

_____

_____

_____

_____

_____

_____

MAJOR MILESTONES

When you love to run _____

_____

_____

_____

_____

_____

_____

_____

When you first used a spoon _____

_____

_____

_____

_____

_____

_____

_____

_____

MAJOR MILESTONES

When you first tried to climb something _____

_____

_____

_____

_____

_____

_____

_____

When you made a friend _____

_____

_____

_____

_____

_____

_____

_____

WHAT YOU SAID

The first phrase you ever said

_____

_____

Your favorite phrase to say

_____

_____

Words you like to repeat

_____

_____

How you say your name

_____

_____

Words you struggle to say

_____

_____

YOUR FAVORITE THINGS

Your favorite song

_____

_____

Your favorite toy

_____

_____

Your favorite thing to eat

_____

_____

Your favorite game to play

_____

_____

Your favorite type of day

_____

_____

A LETTER TO YOU AT TWO

LOOKING BACK ON YOUR SECOND YEAR

When I used to read fairy tales, I fancied that kind of thing never happened, and now here I am in the middle of one!

—LEWIS CARROLL

YOUR CHILD IS THREE!

Look who's three! The toddler years are in full swing. You have most likely seen major milestones occur in these first three years, which makes this part of the book so unique. So much starts to happen now.

In this section, you will be able to record the adventurous moments and silly, mischievous behavior. You will also find dedicated prompts to help you reflect on the feelings and emotions amassed throughout this year of your child's life. This section includes pages filled with categories encouraging you to share the details of your child's third birthday celebration, major milestones, and other fun times. This book already contains such important recorded moments that you can look back on with fondness. Keep going—there's so much more to tell!

CELEBRATING YOUR THIRD BIRTHDAY

How you celebrated your birthday

_____

_____

Gifts you received

_____

_____

Favorite foods you ate

_____

_____

People who celebrated with you

_____

_____

Fun things you did that day

_____

_____

The toddler years are here! How would you say your day-to-day experience with your child differs from the last few years? Are there ways in which they're similar? Share some examples of these moments.

_____

_____

_____

_____

_____

_____

_____

_____

_____

_____

_____

_____

_____

_____

_____

The emotional journey for parents changes a lot from the newborn days to the toddler years. What are some new thoughts and feelings you have experienced lately?

_____

_____

_____

_____

_____

_____

_____

_____

_____

_____

_____

_____

_____

_____

_____

_____

Has parenting your child been what you expected, or is raising a three-year-old very different from what you initially anticipated? What has surprised you most? Has anything been disappointing?

_____

_____

_____

_____

_____

_____

_____

_____

_____

_____

_____

_____

_____

_____

_____

What parenting resource has helped the most? A friend? A book? A podcast? Describe some of the things you're learning and where you're learning them from.

_____

_____

_____

_____

_____

_____

_____

_____

_____

_____

_____

_____

_____

_____

_____

_____

_____

MAJOR MILESTONES

When you dressed yourself _____

_____

_____

_____

_____

_____

_____

_____

When you like to dance _____

_____

_____

_____

_____

_____

_____

_____

_____

MAJOR MILESTONES

When you tried to ride a tricycle _____
_____
_____
_____
_____
_____
_____
_____

When you played pretend _____
_____
_____
_____
_____
_____
_____
_____
_____

MAJOR MILESTONES

Some of your favorite sports or games _____

_____

_____

_____

_____

_____

_____

How you've tried getting yourself dressed _____

_____

_____

_____

_____

_____

_____

_____

MAJOR MILESTONES

The simple directions you can follow _____

_____

_____

_____

_____

_____

_____

_____

How potty training is going _____

_____

_____

_____

_____

_____

_____

_____

WHAT YOU SAID

The "why" questions you've asked

_____

_____

The objects you can identify

_____

_____

The number of words you can say

_____

_____

A song you can sing

_____

_____

A story you like to tell

_____

_____

YOUR FAVORITE THINGS

Your favorite places to go

_____

_____

Your favorite places to eat

_____

_____

Your favorite people to see

_____

_____

Your favorite object or toy

_____

_____

Your favorite book

_____

_____

A LETTER TO YOU AT THREE

LOOKING BACK ON YOUR THIRD YEAR

You have been my friend. That in itself is a tremendous thing.

—E. B. WHITE

YOUR CHILD IS FOUR!

Time to break out the party hats—your child is four, and it's cause for more celebration! What a journey it's been, raising your little baby into a big-kid preschooler. The last several years have been brimming with so many changes. These are some of the most important and formative years your child will encounter. You will remember them too, especially now that details of your child's first years of life have been written and stored in these pages.

Now it's time to describe how your child celebrated their fourth birthday and personalize these memento pages with photos and memories. There are also spaces for you to take the time to stop and reflect on this latest year of parenting, so be sure to capture as many moments as possible.

CELEBRATING YOUR FOURTH BIRTHDAY

How you celebrated your birthday

_____

_____

Your favorite presents to open

_____

_____

The treats you had at your celebration

_____

_____

The people who celebrated with you

_____

_____

Your favorite activity of the day

_____

_____

Your child has done so much growing these last few years. Along with growth, new routines come into play. Have any of these changes affected the way you parent your child? How is it different?

_____

_____

_____

_____

_____

_____

_____

_____

_____

_____

_____

_____

_____

_____

_____

_____

There are days when you look at your child and can almost see glimpses of a big kid. The baby phase is long gone. What significant changes have shown you that your child is quickly growing up?

_____

_____

_____

_____

_____

_____

_____

_____

_____

_____

_____

_____

_____

_____

Each year of your child's life is marked by certain areas of growth or leaps forward in development. Which year of your child's life has been the most fun to watch? Which time or season has been toughest?

_____

_____

_____

_____

_____

_____

_____

_____

_____

_____

_____

_____

_____

_____

_____

Now that your child is preschool age, how do you feel about their education? Will you send them to school? Teach them from home? What are your educational hopes for their future?

_____

_____

_____

_____

_____

_____

_____

_____

_____

_____

_____

_____

_____

_____

_____

MAJOR MILESTONES

Things you like to draw _____

_____

_____

_____

_____

_____

_____

_____

_____

Your favorite place to go _____

_____

_____

_____

_____

_____

_____

_____

_____

_____

MAJOR MILESTONES

Activities you do by yourself _____

_____

_____

_____

_____

_____

_____

_____

Phrases you've been saying lately _____

_____

_____

_____

_____

_____

_____

_____

MAJOR MILESTONES

You're always asking for _____

_____

_____

_____

_____

_____

_____

_____

Your first day of pre-school was _____

_____

_____

_____

_____

_____

_____

_____

MAJOR MILESTONES

How you're learning to brush your teeth _____
_____
_____
_____
_____
_____
_____
_____
_____

Who your friends are _____
_____
_____
_____
_____
_____
_____
_____
_____
_____

WHAT YOU SAID

Funniest thing you've said lately

_____

_____

Your favorite phrase to say

_____

_____

What you say when you're happy

_____

_____

What you say when you're upset

_____

_____

What you say when you're scared

_____

_____

YOUR FAVORITE THINGS

Your favorite thing to do

_____

_____

The toy you love most

_____

_____

Your favorite show to watch

_____

_____

Your favorite song to hear

_____

_____

Your favorite food to snack on

_____

_____

A SPECIAL PLACE WE VISITED TOGETHER

This page is for keeping fun mementos like ticket stubs, wristbands, photos or other keepsakes.

A LETTER TO YOU AT FOUR

LOOKING BACK ON YOUR FOURTH YEAR

You have brains in your head. You have feet in your shoes. You can steer yourself any direction you choose.

—DR. SEUSS

YOUR CHILD IS FIVE!

Your child is five—that's a whole hand worth of fingers! What an adventure for you watching your child grow during this time. You have filled out the pages of this keepsake memory book month after month, year after year. Now you can look back through this book and reminisce about who your child was and who you got to see them become. You can share this book with your child, as well as other loved ones. All those moments are safely stored here for you.

You have reached the final section of this book, where you'll record all the impactful moments of watching your child grow into the next stage of childhood. In the pages ahead, you can document how your child celebrated their fifth birthday, add your child's artwork, and dedicate a letter to your big-kid five-year-old. Congratulations on completing your book! You have a wonderful lifetime ahead of watching your child grow.

CELEBRATING YOUR FIFTH BIRTHDAY

How you celebrated your birthday

_____

_____

Your favorite present to open

_____

_____

The people who celebrated with you

_____

_____

The treat you enjoyed most

_____

_____

The activities or games you played

_____

_____

YOUR ARTWORK FROM THIS YEAR

Stick your favorite artwork here, or get creative and cut and paste a fun collage!

A LETTER TO YOU AT FIVE

LOOKING BACK ON YOUR FIFTH YEAR

REFERENCES

Carroll, Lewis. *Alice's Adventures in Wonderland*. Boston: Lee and Shepard, 1869.

Dahl, Roald. *The Minpins*. New York: Puffin Books, 2009.

Milne, A. A. *The House at Pooh Corner*. London: Dutton, 1961.

Saint-Exupéry, Antoine de. *The Little Prince*. San Diego: Harcourt, 2000.

Seuss, Dr. *Happy Birthday to You!* New York: Random House Children's Books, 2013.

Seuss, Dr. *Oh, the Places You'll Go!* St. Louis: Turtleback, 1990.

White, E. B. *Charlotte's Web*. London: Puffin, 2002.

ABOUT THE AUTHOR

 **Terri McHugh** is a professional photographer and the founder of XOXO terri, a lifestyle and parenting website. As a blogger, Terri has accumulated a social media presence that reaches millions per month. Terri currently resides on the coast of North Carolina with her husband, three children, beagle, and bearded dragon. Through blogging, Terri shares insightful tips she has learned as a mom of three, via parenting hacks, kid-friendly recipes, family travel ideas, and interior design on a budget. Some of her most exciting work includes partnerships with brands like Walmart, KIND, Arhaus, and Macy's. Terri's photography work and recipes have been featured in *The Village* magazine (a quarterly parenting publication) and AllRecipes.com. For the latest lifestyle hacks, follow XOXOterri.com and @terrimchugh on Instagram.

CPSIA information can be obtained
at www.ICGtesting.com
Printed in the USA
BVHW010925231222
654917BV00007B/395